RHYMELESS MUTTERINGS OF A POET

NISHEETA PATNAIK

Made with ♥ on the Notion Press Platform
www.notionpress.com

To my family,

for your nature and nuture.

To my work-spouses and friends,

for just being.

To the foredoomed love of my life,

for all the memories.

Contents

Contents

Contents

Contents

Contents

Contents

Contents

Contents

Preface

I began dabbling in poetry sometime in 2016. But being an English major's daughter and knowing all the rules that *should* go into a poem, I was always hesitant to share. Times have changed from the traditional teachings - it is more accepting & forgiving now. You don't need a rhyme scheme in every one of them. It is a portrayal of your emotions. A description of sensations that in its truest being is intangible. Poetry is a form of art.

I wrote when and where the moment arose. Every surge of emotional reaction would easily be transformed into a string of words. There is no order to the chaos. So, over the years, there were varying themes to the writings. I tried to categorize it for the collection and have segregated it into four parts. Within each part, the works are arranged in chronological order.

A huge part of my life is about the struggles. Struggles with self-doubt, loneliness, the need for perfection, to excel, to beat the odds. About new beginnings, commitment to ambition, adapting to change. It is about how *there is always sunshine after rain* and thustitled *Sunshine Struggles.*

Then there is always love. *Agonizing Amore.* Oh, the devastatingly beautiful thing we let ourselves fall into repeatedly, with all the inevitable heartbreak that follows. The second half of this section I call *Grief.* A cathartic journey of loss – of my love and a bit of myself, and the journey to stabilization.

Harbouring Haven is about home. Home that came to me as my family and as my friends. People who have never left my side. No matter the day, time, or mood. Who read me from across the room and many who were present only digitally, never fail to remind me I am loved and cared for. Framed as birthday wishes, thank you's and goodbyes that were really *see you soons!*

I built the final chunk of my writing when I was in Rishikesh during my post-graduation. There truly is something spectacular about the Himalayas. A sensation that one can only *try* to put into words. This feeble attempt takes form in *Rambling Writer.* Moments where I would be sitting by the Ganges, driving up the serpentine roads, or maybe just gazing out of my window – I have tried to capture with words.

As you read through the collection, I am sure you will note how alliteration, and personification are my favorite literary devices. I hope you enjoy, relate, and derive your own meaning from the writings.

P.S. The book's cover is from a memorable trip to Landour, Mussoorie on Christmas Day 2020. After a crazy night shift in the COVID ICU, a fellow traveller & instagrammer and I drove up to experience the X-mas spirit at Rokbey Manor and the sunset amidst the snow topped mountains. Landour has a piece of my soul. It encompasses all four components of this travelogue – having been there with my family, my love, and my friends on three separate occasions and is the picturesque hill station that has stolen many a heart.

Sunshine Struggles

1. Let me be

Let me be a little while longer,\
Let me snuggle with my teddies.\
Let me play with the benevolent lion,\
Who in reality would chew me out alive.\
Let me be in my warm cocoon,\
Let me hug my little husky.\
Let me indulge in my sweet child-like dreams,\
Because reality is harsher than it seems.\
∞ 16.1.2017

2. Mask

This is your social face.
A face you put on for the world to see.
A look that is bright and full of life.
To show them that
You are happy
Confident
Good
That your day is perfect
Pristine
Beautiful
Not crumbling into pieces inside you
Not shattering into pellets around you
Not piercing your heart & clenching your lungs
So hard that you cannot breathe
Cannot move
Cannot hear
anything above all the deafening noise
All the screaming thoughts
And the murderous silences.
This is the mask you paint on
To comfort them that all is well.
∞ 10.8.2017

3. Clocks that Crumble

Come

Let's go some place brand new

For my shoes are collecting dust

And my soles are getting itchy.

My cam shutters slowing down

My mind is sweetly sedating.

Come

Let's go somewhere unknown,

Before the clock begins to crumble.

∞ 27.8.2017

4. Ringing in the panic

My head is ringing with all this noise.
The ringing is now reverberating
The reverberation now a gyration
The gyration now a blur.

My gut is churning with all this acid.
The churning turns into frothing
The frothing into a liquefaction
The liquefaction now a pulp.

My hand is tingling with all this heat.
The tingling becomes a twitch
The twitching now a palpitation.
The palpitation now a panic.
∞ 28.8.2017

5. Ephemeral

One day it will all come to an end
The joy and the torture alike.
The world will collapse onto itself
Pulling into it every bit of light
Every essence of sound
Plunging us into complete darkness.
So why spend today being someone you are not?
Why spend it doing something you dislike?
Why pine for the boy who didn't love you
Or the girl who repeatedly broke your trust?

Everything you feel is real
Everything you sense is true.
Embrace the turmoil & the torment.
Rejoice in the happyness & the hilarity.
Swallow the indifference & the insensitivity.

Because one day
It will all come to an end
All the apprehension
All the euphoria.
∞ 5.9.2017

6. The Ghostly Night

It's the nights that are hard.
Cold and dreary.
The lights go down and
The imps come out
Whispering terrible tales into my head.
It's the nights that are lonely.
Misty and damp.
The sun sets on me and
The devil turns up
Suggesting venomous yarns into my ears.
Someone turn the switches back on.
I can't have him find me again.
Won't let him dictate my affects
I'm not one of his little puppets
I am grounded. I am sane.
I am drowning. I am pain.
It's the nights that are bitter.
Hurt and fragmented.
The dark settles around me.
Look there he comes
Brewing me a hot cup of madness and rage
∞ 24.09.2017

7. Hideout

I dream of my high school
A place I haven't been for years.
The small three floored building
Covered in chipping blue & white paint.
Can a place bring out a sense of peace?
Nostalgia that brings you to your knees.

~

I dream of my jungle gym
A place I haven't climbed for years.
The then - humungous instalment
Coloured up in bright yellow & red paint.
Do you remember the last time
You hung upside down without worry
about the bloomers under your pinafore?
The last time boys were just people
People who didn't look at you different
who knew you could beat them at the race.

~

I dream of my hideout
A place I haven't snuck up to in years.
The roof top was always under construction
Covered in wastes of white and brown.
A born loner I always had a knack of finding a seclusio

Away from the responsibilities of a 13 year old.

I miss my alfresco safe house

Now I have nowhere to run.

∞ 27.09.2017

8. Matryoshki

I remember spending so much time
wondering
how I would get out of this box
this courtyard
these 4 walls and
Pounce right into the outside world,
Climb over into the real place,
where the grown-ups were.
I remember spending so much time
thinking
about adulthood
the illusion of freedom,
the glory of independence
that I didn't
pay attention
to being cocooned,
to the safety nets,
to the carefreeness.

And here I am
In another box,
Dans la cour de château
Nel grande cortile

Realising that the real world

Is really

a set of reversed Matryoshki.

∞ 3.08.2018

9. The Gruesome & Glorious

It's these nights,
These glorious exasperating hours
That bring out the best of us.

It's these days,
These gruesome beautiful minutes
That teach us the best of lessons.
∞ 01.10. 2018

10. Stand

• 14 •

Stand tall, chin up
Pause & see
The branches holding on
Stop & watch
The mist swooshing by
Halt & sense
All the will inside of you
Stand up, shoulders square 'cause the sky is the limit.
∞ 14.02.2019

11. Kosmos

A few minutes of quiet
Before the confusion of the crowds
Before the maddening of the memsahibs
Before the pandemonium of the patients
A few seconds for me
And the unadulterated Kosmos.
∞ 22.02.2019

12. Universes' Spicule

It's strange

How powerful a photograph is

How fickle words are

& how permanent actions are

But then you remember

You are a tiny spicule

In this ginormous universe.

So sit back relax

Sip your délicieux coffee

& enjoy la comédie show

∞ 23.03.2019

13. Dark Side of the Moon

The clock strikes one, the air still warm
The shutters latched, the crescent smiling.
One day at a time,
A moment to learn something new
A minute to see a different side of you

The clock strikes one, the sky very clear
The gates locked, the first quarter calling
One night at a time,
A twinkle in the deep dark blue
A second to see the other side of you.
∞ 09.06.2019

14. Patience

Patience is a virtue.
True be whoever said so.
Kindness is a boon
For each has their own baggage.
Empathy is an asset
For each has their own troubled path.
Patience is a gift,
To be quiet and forgiving.
∞ 27.07.2019

15. Scarmbled

Sprawling in the humidity
Toying with the food.
A luxurious luncheon at last!
Pay attention to the texture
The egg soft, almost as I like it.
To the spices
The veggies in a perfect mush.
To the sound of
The cricket match from the tele
To the hot air
Swooshing in from the entrance.

Suddenly, laughter rumbles
Thunder behind me
A battery of surgeons
Guffawing over nothing relevant
A rabble of 1ˢᵗ years
scurrying away to their classes
The babies babble before
Bawling during their exam.

The sky is blue, always is.
It pours and shines and dries.

My thoughts are unclear; fidgety,

I could cry I could laugh I could be grateful

All in a moment's notice

Mistakes are made - not to be forgiven

Or to be reminded but to be remembered.

Random, focus, don't drift.

It's lunch time here.

A rare one too

The egg is scrumptious

Sybaritic even

Scrambled though it might be.

∞ 23.08.2019

16. Are You Listening?

Fresh marigolds,
Gush downstream.
Hush little child
You should be wild.
Lush evening skies
Blush the sun dies
Shush little baby
You should be up high

Plush the garden
Swoosh swing goes
Scream out kid
You should be heard.
∞ 25.10.2019

17. Avant la tempête

• 22 •

Beautiful silences
Deafening quietness
Pseudo peace
Calm before the storm.
Dreadful silences
Uncomfortable reticence
Fraudulent harmony
Calm before the calamity
Deceitful silences
Unsual quiescence
Fictitious quietude
Let's prepare for war.
∞19.11.2019

18. Dzogchen

Faithful, love you.
Blindly you love.
Truthful tell you
Blue sky above.
Graceful feel you
Quiet moment hove
Grateful are you
Right now life of

Peaceful are you
Sunset, White dove.
∞ 07.12.19

19. Irréfléchie

Strange windowless walls
Stand front and tall
Ignorant are they
Mindless all say.
Strange purposeless shawls
Shoulder broad and fall
Silly are they
Blindly obey.
Strange counterless stalls
Quietly in thrall
Visionless are they
Far from them stay.
∞ 9.12.2019

20. Fortune de Demain

Through the smoke and mirrors
Emerged a source of light
Beyond the horizon
So strong & so bright
The fog was lifted
The hills with sharp lines
Flowers saturated
Each curve of each dew
Spectacular in the luminance
Glowed with all it's glory
The fortunes of tomorrow.
∞ 31.12.2019

21. Follow

Follow those wisps
Soft & intangible.
Tangled amongst
The crevices.
Steady feet
Left, right then left
Onward march
Up & up
Towards zenith
Follow your desires
Quiet & powerful.
Unraveled inside
The precipice.
∞ 17.1.2020

22. Dark Chaos

Dark Chaos

Unsilent uprise

Ignorant minds

Devious propagandist.

Debilitated hue

Clamorous cry

Asinine heads

Disastrous inculcators.

Dark Chaos

Boisterous bellows

Imbisilic mentums

Destructive promulgation.

∞ 20.3.2020

23. Insignificant

Don't you realise how insignificant we are?
Don't you see the wrath of nature?
Don't you see the walls crumbling down?
Don't you see the gravity of the situation?
Don't you realise how insignificant we are
In spite
Of all the monuments we've created
Of all the lands we've conquered
Of all that we supposedly invented?
Don't you realise how insignificant we are?
Don't you see the preposterous propagandas?
Don't you see the casuistic concoctions?
Don't you see the power of the nincompoops?
∞ 23.3.2020

24. What (did) we sign up for.

There are men outside
Inside gutters
Emptying sludge
With just their hands
and shovels.
Scoop, Lift, Drop, repeat
Scoop, Lift Drop, repeat.

There are women down
Mid March heat
Guarding doors
With just their might
And volition
Stand, Look, Report, repeat.
Stand, Look, Report, repeat.
There are kids on dirt roads
Sunrise till dusk
Rolling tyres
With just their sticks
And stones.
Smile, Play, Eat, repeat

Laugh, Play, Eat, repeat

Our army stands
Allotted station
Anticipation
Wicked this way
Cripple(d) system
Deep Breath, Suit up, Wait, repeat.
Deep Breath, Suit up, Wait, repeat.
Deep Breath, Repeat.
∞ 4.4.2020

25. Skhizein

Eyes closed, hands intwined
Warm tea, cold breeze
Birds chatter, Men banter
Majesties watch silently.
Eyes open, feet steady
Hot 'fe, salt breeze
Horns blaring, 'ple holler
Majesties chim noisily
Two sides, same coin
Four pages, same book
Six songs, same record
Can I be, surely I can.
∞ 15.5.2020

26. Lazaretto

Struggling to bloom
Inside a cocoon
Vacuum & zoom
Lazy afternoon.
Crawling to doom
Growing misfortune
Bed & bath room
Silent classroom.

Strumming tomb
Cordon opportune
Fork table spoon
Desert honeymoon
∞ 31.5.2020

27. Broken B-side

Track 11, 14, 19:
loud ludicrosity, depressed
rude shrew, stranded
cruel callousity, (ex) cluded
Track 22, 24, 27:
solemn gloom, lonesome
babbling baby, abhorred
unsolicited charm, suicidal.
∞ 06.06.2020

28. Grow Up

No care in the world
Race down the alley
Panting, grinning,
Screaming, "I win! I win!"
Barely 3 years old
Hardly 3 feet high.
Universe in your hands.

Outgrew those shoes
Tighten the screws
Out shrunk the ruse
The maze, the zoos.

Albatross swoops low
Threatening to woe
Panting, grunting
Shouting, "You wouldn't dare"
Easily 50 years old
Surely 6 feet high.
Shields up, your hands.
∞ 12.08.2020

29. Vers l'avant

Forward, don't look back.
Strings pull, firm control.

One foot then the next,
A fist over the other.

Skyward, don't look down
Road curves, cruise course.

One crossroad then the next,
A home over another.

Leeward, don't mess up
Taut ropes, steady fall.

One bridge then the next,
A memory over the other.
∞ 05.09.2020

30. Sane

Difficult are people
Difficult are times
Sane we must stay
One time one day.

Feet on the ground
Clear head, no sound.
Sane we must stay
Soon we will be okay.

∞ 12.9.2020

31. Grey

Who declared
Heavens above
Hell down below.

Who decided
Happy smiles
Hatred frowns.

Who testified
Hopes glorify
Calvary curses.

Who prophesied
Good betides
Bad departs.
∞ 04.10.2020

32. Glacier Blue

Blue again
Melting ice
Rolling dice
Smile, the pain.

Blue again
Rotating sun
Relapsing run
Beguile, the bane.

But she's blue again
Bile and shame
Pride and game(s)
Time to shift lanes.
∞ 23.10.2020

33. Box

Moonlight streaks
Across the floor
Cigarette smoke
Perfume galore.

Cooler rustle
Across the hall
Ghosts long lost
Futures past call.

Views confine
Across the window
Our box world
C'we really go?
∞ 02.11.2020

34. Ides

Beware Beware
The Ides is here
Can't you hear him sneer?

From the tip of my nose
To the end of the road
There's nothing but oblivion.

Beware Beware
The Ides is passing
Is that him sighing?

Walk until the shore line
To the end of the road
It's just white oblivion.

Beware Beware
The Ides has gone
Can't you hear him crying?
∞ 15.03.2021

35. Résiliente

Broken to be made again.
Torn down to grown again.
Thrown to be sown again.
Smelted to be moulded again.
Stretched to be pulled up again.
∞ 3.4.2021

36. Knots

Tummy knots
Tongue tie
Watch wind sigh.

'tertwine paths
Swish by
Watch plan fly.

Sunset blots
Fade shy
Watch shade die.

Forget me nots
Bewitch cry
Watch still I lie
∞ 17.05.2021

37. Grieving Hour

Passion elusive
Means to an end.
Progress indecisive
Two steps back send.

Sunlight filter
Curtains as leaves
Seconds glitter
Time quietly grieves.

Chaos clutter
Upheaval dismay.
Brittle bones shatter
Away I stray.
∞ 18.5.2021

38. Ciel Vif

Look, the sunrise
Shift colours bright
Banish dark dawn
Little stars fade.

Look, the new day
Shift mindsets right
Clear clutter sight
Turn vivid shade.
∞ 21.5.2021

39. Lamp

Light you a lamp
All these feelings.
Hold my hand
Need help, leaning.

Light you a lamp
Ask, receiving.
Question, demand
Don't stop breathing.

Light you a lamp
Hope and healing.
Hold your hand
Never be leaving.
∞30.5.2021

40. Unbelievable

Unbelievable is it
The path I've travelled
Turn back time
Invigorate thy younger self.

Unbelievable is it
The lives I've see
Slow down time
Strengthen my present soul.

Unbelievable is it
The curves that lay ahead
Can't stop time
Galvanize forthcoming spirits.
∞ 14.7.2021

41. Now

Auto pilot into the sunset
Scenes change a blink
Forever now
Now forever.
No tomorrow
Isn't that clever?

Cruise slow into the sunlight
Weather stays same.
Seconds moving
Move the second
Now a fraction
Easy to reckon?

Drive away into the sunrise
Motifs morph melt
Now infinite
Infinite gone
No beginning
Time be reborn?
∞ 31.7.2021

42. Balance Essential

Towers over mountains
Suppose bit of both
Balance essential.

Mountains over plains
Above not below
Best of all worlds.
∞ 7.08.2021

43. Murky Minds

Difficult mind
Murky water
Unclear view
But be kind.

Leave behind
Foggy skies
Blurry queues
Quiet down mind.
∞ 08.08.2021

44. Sow

How do you leave a place like this?
Torn between the nomadic
& the urgent urge to settle.
How do you let your roots sow?

How do you leave a place like that?
Tossed between the comforts
& the urgent urge to grow.
How do you let your roots sow?
∞ 20.10.2021

45. Free-bound

Body bind
Ankles cinched
Wrists tied
Struggle sighed

Water body
Fluid move
Run loose
Freedom cried
∞ 31.10.2021

46. Let's Play

Hidden in plain sight
The blue, the green, & white
Come let's play hide & seek
Oh please don't be so bleak.

Hidden in plain view
The cocoa coffee brew
Let's play peek-a-boo
Oh don't broth in that stew.

There right under your nose
The lillies, jasmine, and rose
Wanna play snakes & ladders?
Maybe before everything shatters
∞ 14.11.2021

47. Very Well

Not doing very well.
Mess-a-room
Creased clothes
Unkempt eyebrows
What proper meal?
There I said it out loud.

Not doing very well.
Easy to pen
To faceless profiles
Inappropriate reactions
What judgement!
Hear hear you don't know.
Not doing very well.
Grateful truly
Roof and food
Clean clothes
Fulfilled job
What a life?
There something incomplete.

Not doing very well
Cloudy days

Shady plays
Sunshine peeks out somewhere
What a whirlwind!
There there it will get better.
∞ 17.11.2021

48. Drive

Into the unknown
Roads long and lovely
Winding and twisting
Leading somewhere.

Into the darkness
Repeat routine mundane
Tortuous and turvy
Moving nowhere

Into the sunset
Route scenic & serene
Curving and turning
Always forward.
∞ 28.11.2021

49. Serene Solitude

Beautiful lonliness
Quiet solitude
Never understood
Negative annotations
Behind the isolate

Beautiful lonliness
Serene solitude
Felt understood
Positive allocations
Safely in isolation.
∞19.12.2021

50. Sun Downer

• 57 •

Watch the sun go down on your troubles, but the dark let's the demons out.

Watch the sun go down on your troubles, but let the sleep drown the noise out.

Watch the sun go down on your troubles, but it will surely rise again tomorrow.

∞ 6.2.2022

51. Fields of Lily

I will find you
Amongst the spider lilies.
Wandering about
Swaying with the wind.

I will find you
Amongst the palm forests
All by yourself
Struggling with the mud.

I will find you
Amongst the starry skies
Surrounded by love
Embellishing your crown.

I will find you
Amongst the spider lilies.
Wandering about
Swaying with the wind.
∞ 14.02.2022

52. Unceasing

Roads never end

Stories don't write

Themselves

Horizons can't capture

Clouds don't hold

Water.

Oceans not still

World won't stop

Moving

Roads never end

Stories won't write themselves.

∞ 13.3.2022

53. The Tree

Symbol of timely season
Notion of perseverant resilience
Reminder of beautiful strength
Nature, by extension - you are
You are as much nature
As is the tree.
∞ 29.3.2022

54. Temporary

Tumbling through time
Cruising through crowds.
Strange is this life
With its temporary
Flowers, showers and clouds.
∞ 31.3.2022

55. Trudging

There goes the steam roller
Slowly trudging down the highway.
White noise from the rain outside
Fills up the entire bedroom.

There goes 'nother Sunday
Slowly sneaking down the streets
Music & dialogue blaring through
Fills up the empty household.

There goes my feet , one two
Slowly plodding through puddles
Chitter chatter and howling babies
Fills up the days to come.
∞ 31.7.2022

Agonizing Amore

56. Right Here

Gimme a call, cause I'm right here
Come drop by, cause I'm right here
Knock on my door, cause I'm right here
Hold out your hand, cause I'm right here.
Gimme a min of your day,
Come let's go for that show.
Open your arms wide open,
Hold my fingers, all ten of them.
The rain won't slow,
neither will time.
But you do know
That the sun will shine
So, take a moment and
Drop me a line, 'cause I'm right here.
Hold my hand, 'cause I'm right here.
∞ 15.07.2017

57. Knowning You

For in my heart of hearts,
I already know you.
I have been with you for years
I've seen you long before we met
I know your cracks, gaps
Wounds and scars.
Your laughter seems so familiar
Your smile so comforting
The flicker of anger so natural.

But I don't know you
I don't know who you are
I don't know the things you've been through
Pains you've felt and endured
Love you've touched and fallen for
I don't know your deepest secrets or lies
Your dreams or your desires.

But somewhere
In my heart of hearts
I know you.
∞ 10.08.2017

58. Empty

I'm soaking head to toe.
The downpour is unkind today.
Trees lashing, grass drooping
The park is empty
Obviously.
I'm submerged brain to heart.
The cloudburst is uncalled for today.
Hands quivering, body shivering.
My anchor is unhinged
Obviously.
I'm drowning mind to soul.
The deluge is inhumane today.
Doors slamming, windows shattering.
The house is abandoned
Obviously.
∞ 29.8.2017

59. Shackles

When will you
Stop saying what you don't mean
And not doing the things you say you will.
When will you
Start the life you so passionately talk about
And stop letting the shackles chain you down.

When will you
Grab the ropes of the metaphorical sails of life
And steer yourself away from that quick sand.

When will I
See those big brown droopy eyes
And hold the hands that heal my heart's pains.

When will you
Finally get onto that blue & white aeroplane
And let your heart find its way back to me
∞ 7.9.2017

60. Come Hither

Come here, let me slip
my fingers under your sleeve.
Let me wrap your arm
like you belong to me.
Come here, let me feel
your essence in the air.
Let me drown in your breath
In all of your despair.
Come here, let me hear you
Ramble on of life & such.
Let me watch them dance
Your eyes I love very much.
Come here, let me steal you
To lands you've never been.
Let me show you
All the world's you haven't seen.
Come here, let me write you
Yet another love song.
Let me possess you
Like I haven't in so long.
∞ 10.9.2017

61. Broken Hearts

We are all broken hearts & bleeding scars.
Bruised over the years
We are all lonely sighs & screaming souls.
Wounded over lifetimes.

You can't save me.
Only I can.
∞ 14.09.2017

62. Flat Line

How do you know it is time to stop?

Is there a end of school bell?

A siren maybe?

Perhaps one last shock,

One more mouth to mouth.

I could bring it back to life.

How do you know it's stopped breathing?

When has it flat lined?

When is it time to let go?

∞ 16.09.2017

63. I'm Sorry

I'm sorry for whatever is hurting you.
I'm sorry I can't fix it.
I'm sorry no one can see the agony
I'm sorry no one is listening.

I'm sorry for whatever broke you.
I'm sorry I can't mend it.
I'm sorry no one can see the pain.
I'm sorry we are all so alone.
∞ 20.09.2017

64. Implicit

How strange
Is this world
Filled and forced
With relationships

How peculiar
Are these men
Made and broken
By association.

How tragic
Is this life
Dumb and Delphic
With all that's unsaid.

∞ 21.11.2017

65. Quiet Conversation

Have you ever had this elaborate conversation with someone,
Absolutely perfect
On the brink of poetic
With the most congruous come backs and the relevant retorts
But it was all in your head?

And when you talk in reality,
you realise you were in love with a version of them.
A version of the perfect person you wish you had
A form that maybe you made up in your mind.
Almost leaves you a little heartbroken.

Maybe I should go back to keeping quiet
Not asking
Not wanting
Let these conversations stay imaginary
Keeps everyone happy that way, doesn't it?
∞ 6.12.2017

66. Tearing Apart

My heart is breaking
Can you hear it tearing at the seams?
I can't make it stop.
Plug in one hole and
it rips through another
Stitch up one end and
it slits out the other.
My heart is shattering
Can you see all the smithereens?
I don't know how to stop.
∞ 30.12.2017

67. Dreamland

You know how in a dream
There isn't a beginning
There isn't an end
Just this middle
Everlasting story that just is.
A tale that has been and forever will be?
That's how it is with you.
A dream of sorts.
∞ 11.1.2018

68. Dream

It's a dream I know
A dream I'm living.
The air so cold &
The skies so clear.
It has to be a dream.
Lost in paradise
Are we together?
Lost apart
Forgetting what's real?
Denial is child's play
Delusions are effortless.
It's a fantasy I know
An illusion I'm living.
The heart is quiet &
The head sublime.
It has to be a dream.
∞ 17.01.2018

69. Tête-à-tête

There are these things I want to say
To you
My little heart's desires.
Everything I thought we could be
Maybe everything we were.
There are these memories I want to share
With you
My teeny mind conjures
Every conversation we've had
Maybe in some other lifetime.
There are these questions I want to ask
Of you
My nimble hands create
Of moments in your life
That I was never a part of.
There are these stories I want to narrate
To you
My silly head remembers
Alas I can't and won't, instead
I'll watch the mumblings wane.
∞ 23.01.2018

70. Pour toujours

Here -
Take my heart
Take a piece
Take it whole
Just take it.
Crystal & pristine
Of shatter-full glass
It's all yours,
Eternally.

All I ask for
Is that you stay
By my side
Forever more.
So here -
Take mon coeur
Unabridged & complete
Pour toujours.
∞ 19.09.2018

71. Laconic moments

When the days seem numbered
Every second resembles precious nectar.
You wish you could bathe in it
Head to toe, arm to ankle, nose to knee
Drench down and drown in it.
When the clock counts down
When the sun sets faster than it rises
When the moon is all we have
Let's count the stars through the night
Let's catch fleeting clouds & fleeing birds
Let's cuddle inside the frozen snow castle
Play hide & seek with father time
When our moments seem compendious
And every wink resembles a lost eternity
Let's whisk away together
Far up in the cold mountain air.
∞ 02.11.2018

72. Love Song 1809

You are the sunshine to my eye
Pretty starlight in the sky
Soft wet breeze of mid July
Darling, smile don't sigh.
You are the sailor to the land
Tippie toes in damp sand
Bright bows to my head band
Precious, hold my hand
You are the bumble to my bee
Strange bristles of the tree
Fluffy clouds on a spree
Mon cher amour sourire
∞ 18.09.2019

73. Glance

Gushing from one end
To end
Brushing finger tips
One 'other
Singular second
Stolen stare
Encompass all
Unsaid.

~

Floating from here
To there,
Twinkling bright eyes
See 'other
Discrete dates
Pinched peeks
Bellowed all
Unspoken.

~

Darting left and
Then right
Smirking soft lips
Smile 'other

Inaudible infatuation

Grazed glances

Veiled all

Cupidity.

∞ 14.2.2020

74. Forever Moments

A fraction of a min
Sky clear
Sun shines
River shimmers
A fractal of a second
Hands meet
Eyes seek
Hearts beat.
A slice of silence
Chunk of change
Portion of prophecies
Amalgamate
Tether these
Eternal entities.
∞ 22.2.2020

75. Lonely Hearts

Independent organ are you
Born alone, destined to be
Incomparable
World filled with
Lonely souls
Broken bowls
Haywire controls

Sovereign spirit are you
Born mighty, designed to be
Indomitable
Universe overflows with
Reclusive residents
Crippled repents
Chaotic laments.
∞ 28.3.2020

76. Endless

An endless winter
Tragedy
Shrivelled trees
Chilly breeze
Weeping heart.

An endless spring
Agony
Dwindled tears
Irrational fears
Lonesome depart.
An endless summer
Melancholy
Faded letters
Unchained fetters
Cuore fall apart .

An endless monsoon
Catastrophe
Foggy forecast
Ashamed aghast
Arduous start.
∞ 02.04.2020

77. Lingering Ghosts

Wish I had taken more
Unruly haired pictures
Proper posture advices
Chocolate banana smoothies
(ok maybe no)

Wish I had given more
Minutes of the day
Deluxe head massages
Oven baked veggies & potatoes.

Wish I could hold onto
Your soft lingering smell
Imprints of your body
And the ghosts of your figurine.
∞ 11.07.2021

78. Thoughts of The Day

• 88 •

Today I saw a boy
Pink shirt and sweatpants
Thought it was you.

Today I saw a murmuration
Red sky and white clouds
Thought it could be us.

Today I saw the hills
White haze and cream towers
Thought we could go there.
∞19.07.2021

79. Trivial

How simple, the mind
The desires it shines
Away it goes
Castle cards blow

How simple, the heart
The wants it charts
Show of hand
Slip away sand.

How simple, this life
The plans it knife's
Etched in stone
Unpredictable
Alone.
∞ 29.8.2022

80. Agony

How much it aches
You in agony.

How I wish
I could soothe all
Your suffering

How much it aches
You writhing in pain.

How I wish
Let me in to take
Away your disdain.

How much it aches
You walking on.

How I wish
You could see me
right here.
∞ 5.9.2022

81. Wallow

So unreal
are the storms
the clouds
that follow.
So intangible
are the worries
the troubles
that wallow.
∞ 6.9.2022

82. Amongst all the noise & silence

Everyone has
something to say
Everyone has a
Perspective
Everyone has a
Story to tell
Everyone has a
View to impose
Everyone has a
Voice to share.

Except you.
∞ 14.9.2022

83. Webs

In this vast oasis
Of nothingness
I am caught
In the web
Of extravagant words

One step forward
My ankles jerk back
Webs around my wrists
Hold me tight
Let me go
Let me through
Stuck in time
Stuck in a loop

In this vast oasis
Of nothingness
I am caught
In the web
Of extravagant words
∞ 21.9.2022

84. Chinese Whisperers

Words written
Words spoken
Words misspelt
Words misinterpreted

In the end
Just words
Letters of an
Arbitrary language
Of these
Chinese Whisperers
Meaning nothing

Sounds aloud
Sounds up and around
Sounds misheard
Sounds mistold

These Chinese Whisperers
Love their games.
∞ 23.9.2022

85. Unsaid 106

For all the things I want to tell you,
You deserve nothing.
You deserve the wrath of all the 10 forms of Durga.

For all the things left unsaid,
You deserve none
Even my silence is too expensive for you.
∞ 6.10.2022

86. Time to Stop

Time has past
Stop all the noise
Plug my ears
Scream
Scream over my lungs
Stop all the noise
Stop gnawing
at that wound
It's beyond repair.
Let it heal
Let it breath
Time has passed
But there is so
much more to come.
∞ 9.10.2022

87. Pine

This world
Is filled with
Broken hearts &
Broken dreams.
We cry for
futures that never
came true.
Till then
we shall pine at
the beautiful moon.
∞ 11.10.2022

88. Clear Grey Skies

Path ahead looks grey
But the storm
Will clear soon.

Close your eyes
Listen to the sounds
That ground you
Chugging train
Chirping birds
Cooing pigeons
Tantrums of the child
Tip top blop of the
Make shift waterfall

Path ahead looks grey
But the storm
Will clear soon.
Close your eyes
And breathe
One two three.
∞ 20.10.2022

89. A Quiet

A quiet falls over me
My phone's been silent
The noise doesn't bother

A quiet surrounds me
My mind has been calmer
The chaos doesn't bother

A quiet is in me
Hearts stopped pounding
The beats are rhythmic again.
∞ 21.10.2022

90. Fighting Stance

Sprawled on the floor
Feet ice cold
Cheek to the ground
Fallen hard
Barley breathing

Leaning on the wall
Chin bent down
Palms to the sill
Standing still
Incessant crying.

Left foot forward
Arms up drawn
Shoulders squared out
I'm ready, next round.
Bells-a-ringing
Is that really all you've got?
∞ 28.10.2022

91. No One Told Me

No one really tells you
About the pain
How to untangle that knot
In the middle of your chest
As if something you
swallowed won't move further.

No one really tells you
About the blocks
How to stop all the noise
Inside your head
As if someone left the radio
on the worst news channel.

No one really tells you
About the blurriness
How to clear through the mist
In front of your eyes
As if someone left the shower
And broke off the handle.

No one really tell you
About the hands

All the hands that
Hold you up
Pull you over
All the voices that
Play the advice you know
You would have given
All the words
That would save you
From yourself.
∞ 31.10.2022

92. Smile Today

While the sisters at work
Tugged at my hair
Giggled at my silly jokes
I smiled today
While papa at the door
Shouted out instructions
On how to breathe
Thru the anxiety
I smiled today
While mama on the screen
Wide eyed and gleeful
About the next Amazon purchase
I smiled today
While m msged me
Big sister and all that she is
Life's philosophies
(While going through her own)
I smile today.
While my friends far and wide
Hold my hand virtual & live
I smile today.
∞ 7.11.2022

93. Self Love

Always a loner
The past few months
The last thing I've wanted
The past few days
Stuck in my (conjunctivitis) Qtine
I am no longer scared.
Scared to be with myself
Alone with my thoughts
Or just to love me again.

Trying to understand
Emotional (in)dependence
The core of which
I now presume
Is self love.
Self sufficient-ness
Being your own
Rock, safe place
Best cheerleader.
∞ 18.11.2022

94. That's Okay

The East wind blows
Winter is rolling in again
Clock continues clicking
Wish you were here

The morn fog sweeps
It's November again
Clock continues ticking
Alas you aren't here
But that's okay.

The East wind blows
Winter is rolling in again
Clock continues blinking
I am here right now
And that's okay.

∞ 19.11.2022

95. Proud

Proud I am of myself
Strong & tall I have stood
Still a few downpours I've had
A long way I have come
A long way I have to go
Proud I am of my life
Strong & tall I stand.
∞ 22.1.2023

96. Fickle Mind

The minds a fickle creature
She forgets so easily
The good the bad the ugly
Everything's effervescent

She could rewrite a memory
Change the narrative
The twists the turns the topsys
Momentary minutes

The minds a fickle creature
She barely remembers
The ups the downs the in betweens
Past (im)permanence

The minds a fickle creature
Veridical or volatile
Let me immortalize them
In a picture or a poem.
∞ 29.1.2023

97. Heavy Heart

Heavy heart
unburden thy pain
Long shouldered
Nothing left gain

Heavy heart
Release clenches
Palms bleeding
Get out trenches.

Heavy heart
Open thy eyes
Cheeks tearing
Forever 'byes.
∞ 9.2.2023

98. Nights

Nights like these
Confuse and amaze me
How trivial
Comedy of errors.
Amidst the hum of humanity
We trudge on
Forward March
Forever moving
Through nights like these.
∞ 4.3.2023

99. Poetic Similes

These lines
My mind
Convoluted
Confused.

These lights
My soul
Bright
Diffuse.

The night sky
My life
Blanket darkness
Full of limitless muse.
∞ 11.03.2023

100. Closure

Such a silly concept
Lost in books, movies
But then I've liked
Those with open endings
Mystery ever so tantalizing
Possibilities endless.

Living the open ending is
Terrifying.
Do I really want this line of
Continuity?
How much is in my hands?
Does the writer above
Hold all the puppeteer strings?

Such a silly concept
This closure
Non-existent really
But then I've always loved
Ones with debatable endings
Mysteries ever so riveting
Possibilities oh so limitless
∞ 21.3.2023

101. I Am - A Self Portrait

I am

Independence

Creativity

Femenina

I am

Grounded

Principled

Tempered

I am

Unapologetic

Surgeon

Empath

I am

Growing

Learning

Focused.

∞ 26.3.2023

102. Consistent Trivia

Strange little trivia
Stuck in my head
Highway mirages
Colours of the sky
Hot humid days
The way the night sky paves.

Strange little trivia
Stuck in my brain
Over water bridges
Contrasting sunsets
Mango showers
The movement of the flower.

Strange little trivia
Stuck in my skull
Inclined curves
(In) Consistent clouds
Rainbows after rain
The Sun will always rise again.
∞ 2.4.2023

103. Empty Heartbreak

• 114 •

Heartbreak is
The sound of
An empty house
The quiet of
Squabbling couples

Heartbreak is
Lying on the sofa
'cause the bed's too big.
Throwing out
The lemon tea & coffee.

Heartbreak is
Endless conversations
Everyone else's problems
The loneliness over
Up in the mountain air.

Heartbreak is
The sound of
An empty home
∞ 12.4.2023

104. Remember Remember

Some days I nurture
The ball of pain
That now fits perfectly in
The palm of my hands

Some days I sit
On the floor
By the front door
Poking at the wounds
Watching it bleed

Somedays I stand
In the kitchen
Staring at the oven
Burning all that grief

Some days I press
rewind to remind
That silent Sundays
Are better than
Manic monday mornings.
∞ 7.5.2023

105. The Swansong

Ashamed
Of my (in)dependence
Pitiful
Of my own plight
Clingy
To your presence
Guilty
Of my freedom
Questioning
My rationality.

Oh 'darling',
don't you see
All that
you lost
All the games
mean nothing
Now that
Storm has cleared
Ship has steered
Nothing
Left to be feared.

How dare you
Possess power
To easily trigger
Every stage in grief
Textbook reaction
Funeral for the dead

Oh but 'love'
Don't you see
It's a you problem
Not one bit of me.
∞ 6.6.2023

Harbouring Haven

106. The City

The sky is gloomy and the path muddy
But oh how much she missed it.
So what of the heaps and hills,
The city had stolen this girl's heart.

The roads are chock-a-block and the air heavy
But the speed of life just tangible.
So what of the sleep and slumbers
The town was only her temporary lover. .

The winds are wailing and the floors wet
But the towers are trembling beauties.
So what of the rivers and ravines
The marine essence was all she yearned.

∞ 14.07.2018

107. Lumos

A day to remember
A day to celebrate
The life of someone
Who so easily
brightens all of ours.
Forever smiling
Forever twinkling
Ever grateful are we
That you bring so much
happiness to the world.
Stay blessed
Stay charming
The light that you have
Unfathomable force
That you are,
Always remember
Always celebrate
All the glory
That is you.
∞ 19.02.2019

108. Parcel to Go

Pack me a bottle of petrichor to go
Like all the goodies you've stuffed into my bag.
Pack me a cassette of your morning chatter
Like all the letters you've sneaked into my purse
Pack me a painting of the hill station view
Like all the love you give me u conditionally.
Pack me a piece of home
Because it's time to go be an grown-up again.
∞ 30.06.2019

109. Joyeux Anniversaire '19

The road is treacherous
Heart wrenching
View at the end of it
Breathless cold air
Swirls through the trees.

The cafe is bustling
Giggling girls
Music of an era gone by
Fresh ground coffee
Swirls through the door.
This life is all mine
A year older
Silence drowns out the noise
Ghost of birthday past
Swirls in to say hello.
∞ 29.11.2019

110. Celebration 4019

Two pearly digits
Years forward fidget
Stories unravel
Mountain travel
Playful dreams
Celebratory screams 'Hurrah - hurray
Its your birthday!' Two pearly digits
Deep soul & spirit
Feet over gravel
Eyes forever dazzle
Over to the streams
Celebratory screams 'Hurrah - hurray
It's your birthday!
∞ 19.04.2020

111. Forever Twenty Two

Paradisiacal poet
Ritualistic writer
Furious & feisty
Stubborn psyche
Childish chider
Grounded guide
Greatness personified
Stand still time
Cannot rewin(d)
Here is our babalú
Forever Twenty two
∞ 22.4.2020

112. Circle of Life

There goes another
Ship out at sea
White 'chefs wave
Adeiu, o' night.

Deserted bicycles
Empty nests
Broken cocoons
For idle contests.

There go a few more
Birds in the sky
White wings flap
Ciao, o' bright light.

Rekindled flames
Gyrate dice
Emerge ash
The holy circle of life.
∞24.8.2020

113. Clock Struck

Create a family
Away from home
Fill the void
Mundane drone

All the noise
Commotion crowd
Hands together
Cold and loud

Child frolic forever,
Smiles, joy & holly
Clock struck
Clock stuck
Teeny tiny jolly.
∞ 29.11.2020

114. Birthday 1021

Year - stuck at four
One foot outta the door
Hair in disarray
Perpetually on the floor.

Almonds on fire
D'n't settle, only desire
Pimples to portray
Can't help but admire.

Passionate core
Couldn't ask for more
Bowl of crème brûlée
& My baby sister I adore
∞ 10.1.2021

115. Birthday 1921

From Mountains to beaches
Blue skies and peaches
Mind wanders more than your feet
Your heart dances to the drum beat.

From Glorious gardens to constellations
Jasmine flowers and meditation
Breath steadier than my hand
Your sole firm where you stand.

From one year to the next
Mythology prophecies obsessed.
Your wisdom grows with age
Come on, it's time to turn the page.
∞ 19.4.2021

116. Birthday 0224

Tingle spidey senses
No secrets from you.
Your tiny nerve tenses
Fix it, is all you want to do.

Mitochondrial momentum
Know it all you do
Protect us from gruesome
Cuddle and cocoon, you want to.

Woe is a your middle name
Worry worry, you must not.
Every night, sleep's a game
One mom's all we got.

Another year passes by
Don't listen to all they say
Smile, oh young worrier
Make it a perfectly splendid birthday.
∞ 22.04.2021

117. Not a Goodbye.

Close your eyes, Sky's always blue.
Back and forth, home again.
Open your palms, He's always true.
To and fro, miracle He send.

Open your eyes, Moons all bright.
Here and there, always home.
Open your heart, what a sight.
Up and down, s'much you've grown.

Close your eyes, it's not goodbye.
Breathe in and out, silent zen
Open your arms, farewells are a lie.
Knock knock, Look I'm here again!
∞ 31.3.2021

118. Aie

Baby bum massages
Hand feeding me silly.
Devoted deity corsages
Baby sitting frocks frilly.

Story telling relentless
Sharp eyes, a hawk
Loved us condition-less
Elephant mind, cake walk.

Hoarder oh dear galore
Take after you I do.
Remember your snore
Late night TV, black blue.

Should have called more
Written down those recipes
'other day by gopalpur shore
Maybe a story for the road
Alas, it's time for you to go.
∞ 24.4.2021

119. Domicile

Let me tell you a story
A story of a home
A home full of dreams
Dreams who gave us wings
Wings with which we flew
Flew far into the mountains
Mountain peaks in skies blue
But never too far to come back to you.

Let me tell you a tale
A tale of 2 people
People full of hope
Hope that gave us strong feet
Feet with which we ran
Ran far into the sea
See those waves so blue
But never too far to come back to you.
∞ 07.06.2021

120. Kho-Kho

Game of kho kho
Poles and shoulder taps
Back, forward, sideways
Never ending run.

Cobblestone streets
Sanctuary for years
Home, hermitage, haven
Ever shinning sun.

Gazillion goodbyes
Can't get one to stick
Adieu, au revoir, hello!
Forever, my only one.
∞11.06.2021

121. One Day

One sunshiny day
Intersperse sheets of rain
One hot sultry day
In between sighs of pain
One more cosy day
Time to say 'bye again
∞ 14.6.2021

122. She

She stands there
Hand on the rim
Skinny legs crossed
Head titled just a bit
Waving goodbye.

She sits there
Back up against the sofa
Fingers tapping away
Shoulders slouched
Engrossin' games.
She's jumping around
Hammer in hand
Tip toeing on stools
Back a balancing act
Coz it's to be done now.

She stands there
Head on the door
Skinny legs crossed
Proud mama bear smile
Waving goodbye.
∞17.10.2021

123. Bon Anniversaire 1922

Today - truly yours

Not mine, ours or theirs.

Today - declare reign

For you have fought through.

Today - plant flag

For you have climbed forth.

Today - claim throne

The king of your life.

Today - celebrate

Not for me or them

For all the gloriousness you truly are.

∞ 19.4.2022

124. Au revoir

It's yet another goodbye,
Neh, another Au revoir.
'Cause we shall meet again.
Share struggles & victories
Snippets & never ending tales.
So, Au revoir
My warm ambitious friend (& senior)
Can't wait to see you again!
∞31.08.2022

125. A Toast

Here's to the girl with the long lustrous locks
Who walks through the world as if
it were her very own garden
Flowers adorning her crown
Butterflies following her around
So lovely to fall in love with her
Heres to the girl with full cheeks and beautiful smile
Who walks through the world as if
It were her own playground
Laughter garnishing her surround
Spreading happyness around
So wonderful to stay in love with her.
∞ 30.9.2022

Rambling Writer

126. Fleeting Moments

There, the little boy peeps out of his window
He finds the downpour rather unusual.
His friends were all coped up at home
No one was allowed to go out and play.

There, the middle aged maid waddles through
Her pink saree pulled up around her knees
It was time for the next home to be attended
The rains had absolutely no power over her.

There, the man stands with his broken umbrella
With a single silver stalk sticking out
He hugs his backpack as if his life were at stake
As he patiently waits for the leaky red bus to arrive.
There, the old man in the blue wind cheater
Crossing the wide road to reach home.
A sadness touches his face, one that
Spoke stories of many missed minutes.

There, the uniformed guard sits on his plastic chair
Filling his files and pushing the buttons
He seems quiet with the storm that surrounds
He watches the clock, awaiting his time to leave.

There, the petit girl peeps out of her window
She always wanted a life filled with more.
Everything was on pause for a few days and
She intended to imbibe all these fleeting moments.
∞15.07.2018

127. The Flutist's Cairn

I don't see the hills as much as I'd like to.
A late afternoon by the cairn amongst the devotees,
A quiet weekend with the green of the waters and the blue of the sky
I can't think of anything else I need to get by

I don't see the rivulet as much as I'd love to
A breezy après midi on the pebbles amongst the believers,
Peacocks cooing across the waters and the flutist playing his melody
Come, let's sit together and let the whole world be.
∞ 17.11.2018

128. Aventure Exotique

New places with old faces,
Exotic spaces with raw paces
Truly sublime are these worlds
Peculiar the wind life twirls
Come see the spirit ,
Come feel the madness,
The adventure of a lifetime.
∞ 26.01.2019

129. Lost Confluences

The tide of people -
overpowering
The wave moved
in unison –
up the road –
down the slope
Follow the red flag
they said
Hold hands tight
they said
Don't lose one another
they tried.

A monkey cap lay
crumpled outside
The waiting areas full
but chairs empty
Shoulders bumping,
fists pumping
Words thrown, eyes
shown.
A stampede brewing
But the cap was left lost & alone.

She decided to leave him
The slipper abandoned
by his partner
Lay dejected and rejected
Drowning in the
sand and dust
Hopelessly staring at the floor
He never knew how to be by himself
What was his purpose in the world then? .

The loud speaker blared on
Day in & night out
Over worked and under valued
He croaked on about
all the missing people
He screeched on
In hopes to find those lost.
Cards dropped, hands slipped
Phones stolen ; wallets cut.
The speaker was all that lay
Between the lost & found.
∞ 05.02.2019

130. Follow the Maddening Crowd

The unending queues
Beginning at dawn
end disappointingly!
What is it you are looking for?
Is being part of the herd
So, rewarding?
Is following a blind king
That satiating?
What is it you plan to achieve?
Can't you see the puppeteers?
Pulling on feeble strings
Can't you see the pied piper?
Leading with muted pings
Can't you see the show?
The ever-blinding ruse
beginning in the frigid sand
end disconcertingly!
∞ 08.02.2019

131. Apercevoir

Chai Wala misses you
The one day you couldn't
make it for the evening break.
A large smile & humble heart
Is what he offers with his cuppa.

The selfless store keeper
Offers you his lunch.
Just an outstretched hand
a hearty welcome
& a warm conversation.
The mother and her two children
Pack their bags on the sidewalk
The lil' girl squeals with glee
At the sight of the monkeys
While her son takes cover.

The dogs are unhappy
With the बंदर झुंड
The waters are gushing on
The light blazes downward
The dust swirls all around but .

The girls with the matching glasses

Can't take a moment to

Look up from their phones

All the world's passing by, dearies.

Look up.

∞ 04.03.2019

132. Out of Order

Having piping hot tea on blurry borders,
Bus swaying ferociously over sharp corners
The French foreigners needed translation
The youthful gang a little deflation.
Street lights twinkled in the rain
Specular view through the misty pane
Quiet is the mind that sits still
Full is the life that has thrill
∞ 17.04.2019

133. Lingering Leftovers

I left a piece of my heart in the wilderness
Amongst the tall towers and wandering wraiths.
I left a piece of my mind in the mountains
Floating in the clouds above all the consuming chaos.
I left a piece of my soul with the spirits
Dancing to the soothing silence of the zeniths.
∞ 1.05.2019

134. Canvas

How beautiful it is to be so aware.
Aware of the sea of people flowing so relentlessly beside you
Observant of their different faces and emotions.
Passing kitchen after kitchen serving bhaturas the size of human heads.
Conscious of the hot then cool gush of air as you drive by the canal banks
Of the bright hotel lights twinkling as if they were the stars themselves
The new moon sky where the glittering celestials got room to shine.
Squinting through the darkness to get a glimpse of the river
Peering at the homes dotting the hills around it.
Finally you reach the end of line & the bright 'city' lights suck you back to reality.
The neon lights banish all the glorious darkness
The canvas that would help you glow.
∞ 25.05.2019

135. The Hills Have Eyes

The air smells damp with the perineal rain
The mountains shape shift in and out
Like cardboard cut outs on Aladdin's Play
Dirty snow turns into water
Gushing and gurgling;
Rushing and giggling;
Over chalky white rocks,
Surely into the valley.

~

The rocks magnanimous,
shinning slate grey;
With natural scars,
running down their entirety.
The trees gorgeous,
shimmering dark green
Their pinnacles,
staring right into the blue sky.

~

The sky turns purely purple out of the blue
Lines smudged into borders of white clouds
Bright orange the sun was sinking from view .
The terraced meadows
lush and rich,

The farmers unhesitantly
smile and wave
The bus sways gracefully
along the soft curves
Rushing upstream
The slithering river
Light sieves through
leaves of the dense forest
Warming me with
the sense of superior motives

~

How beautiful is this world, with
Its birds & monkeys
Its ravines & rainbows
How powerful is The Mother
A pop to shut your ears
A swish to make you sick
How treacherous are we, lost
In our fights & traumas
In our problems & troubles

~

Forget, its not important
For you are the
Universe in totality.
As long as there is
Force in my feet
Air in my lungs

I will live to see everything
This sphere has to offer
'Cause her magnificence
Is calling for me.
∞ 15.06.2019

136. Pause

Time always slows down in the coffee shop
Amongst the humming humans and clinking cutlery
I peer outside the tall windows at the life of the city
Women in suits, strutting up & down the pavement;
talking rapidly - something at work maybe
Men rushing with tubelights and printers;
Hurrying to get the work done before their shift.
Christian women in their Goanese dresses;
Devouring their midweek ice cream cones
Teenage girls with their teenage guys;
Laughing their heads off - not a care in the world.

Oh how wonderful it is to stop time.
To watch each second move so nonchalantly.
Time always slows down when I'm home
I peer out of my bedroom window at the city lights
We brought the stars to the ground, dear
Twinkling to the beats of the traffic noise
The front door opens to a familiar scent
Of damp cement and pigeon poop.
How magnificent is this city
Where just the sight of people revives you

The smell of the rain thrives you and
The sound of life re-energizes you.
∞ 25.06.2019

137. Quintilis

Fluffy balls of cotton
Emerge from the mighty mountains
Exploding miniature atom bombs
In the ravines of the sky
White streaks of slytherins
Merge over the riveting river
Standing still over the waters
Holy spirits of the nymphs
The downpours of the day
Made all clean green & serene
Purple skies bid adieu to Quintilis
Half the year passed away.
∞ 28.07.2019

138. Nymphadora

Watch her sway
In and out
Watch her waltz
To and fro
Up and over
The light and shores
The nymphadora of the ravine.
White ghost like
Swift and soft
Sitting all quiet
Clean and cool
Beautiful
Darling nymphadora
What dreams you give
What fantasies you spring
All in a moment's passing.
∞ 4.08.2019

139. Twenty Minute Drive

Strutting down the pavement
Chin up, hands in pocket
Take a deep breathe in
The chilly air of the river.

Flowing along the artery
There is so much life, yet
Strange come outdoors
To dive back into virtual realities?

Pausing down the pathway
The couples - old and new
The families - two or three
Receive glances of sheer jealousy.

Sauntering through the street
The boy with the bright red shoes
Matching his girl's lovely rosy lips
A smile and a smirk tied in a bow. .
Ambling along the avenue
Watching the grey haired woman
Watch the sky merge from purple

To pink to grey to jet black.
Lingering for a moment
Behind the syndicate of oldies
Hiding from their distraught wives
Imbibing the beauty of the Ganges.

Traipsing through the trail
Avoiding the eve teasers
And mischief makers
To see the familiar lights
Smeared across the horizon.

Twenty minutes
To walk the length of the drive
Twenty minutes
Of animated Homo Sapiens
Twenty minutes
For inner peace & tranquility.
∞ 24.08.2019

140. Castle in the Clouds

Lonesome heart that sighs
Omen, dark dark sky.
Fearful silly soul
Tearful, heavy Kohl.
Glorious dense deep clouds
Notorious, he screams aloud.
Lonesome girl by fire
Kingdom, look higher.
∞ 28.09.2019

141. End of Day

The moon was smiling at me today.
Sharp white curve against the blue.
The clouds soft, large and bright
Floated around her, carefree & light.
The lone lamp sat quietly by the bay
"Here riverside forever can't I stay?"

The mountains loomed gigantically ahead
The flame danced yellow, blue red.
The crescentic Luna smirks at me
The beautiful night is yet to come.
∞1.10.2019

142. Ce monde étrange

Eerie lands of eerie people
Swamp this town oh so regal.
Puffy clouds of puffy people
Heads higher than the steeple.

Little quiet for the sane,
Much to ask, much in vain?
Pause a moment to ascertain
Prevailing peace or just disdain?

Creepy cats at creepy corners
World filled with sad loners.
Stale society, stale conformers
Stay still with your pseudo armours.
For it's a strange world
with strange folk.
∞ 07.10.2019

143. Ramblings of a Writer 1101

My fingers tap nervously on the keys
Mind rushing like busy bees
So much to make, there's hardly any time.

Small feet trudge on the roof above
A rat, cat or dog, I can't tell.
Loud noises from the next room
Over spilled milk? Or ruined silk?

I want to write, I want to create
Something in form, Somewhat with rhythm
But then my mind goes
Wandering, jinxing
The things I have
The luck that prevails
The 'happiness' that surrounds.

Mind is wonderful.
Powerful
Mental.
I can read yours,
sometimes better than you

I want to help you,
but I don't know how to.
Maybe I'm the one who
Needs the push,
To find myself
To place my feet
As grounded as I seem,
Still can't figure out whether
Its land or water that I see.

'You' are the amalgamation
Of people I meet
People I trust
Who leave.

'You' is everyone
Gracing past my life
Everyone who makes an impact
Or I hope would make one.

'You' are this potato mash of a person
Who reminds me
Time and again
That I am enough.
As are you.

Billie Eilish on blaring speakers

Floats down to the windows.
Stale cuppa tea sits on the table
Dim light slithers in the screens.
The wax is dripping off
The purple glass I gave you.
No fragrance sadly,
Just the comfort of the flame.
Comfort of the warmth
The fire that will never disappoint.
∞ 5.11.2019

144. I Spy

I spy a shooting star
For a fraction of a second
Zoom woosh zap!
It made no sound.
I spy a shooting star
In the wee hours of the morn.
Petit white streak
On a cerulean back drop.
I spy a shooting star
When the moon was her brightest
Wish upon it
Not anything I desired.
Wish upon it
Nothing I required
I spy a shooting star
A peek at Aurore
Wish upon her
Reasons to smile
Wish upon her
Good humour & laughter
Wish upon her
A life of contentment.
∞ 17.11.2019

145. Bye Bye November

If I had all the money in the world,
I would have a library
As large as a football field
Filled with gazillion books
I would take twice as many lifetimes to read.

If I had all the luxuries in the world,
I would have a private plane
As free as a soaring seagull
To take me to all the places
I would need thrice as many lives to reach.

If I had all the magic in the world,
I would have a Time Turner
As fluid as Hermione
To live & relive twenty nineteen
I had but one year to realize.
∞ 30.11.2019

146. Shifting Seconds

The hills adorned with green tree tops
Each curve shape shifting every second.
The river is dry , construction is on
Piles of sand mimicking the hills behind.
Like toddlers attempting to .. well toddle.
The girls are bickering, men are snickering
Street dogs shivering, camera's picturing.
Raindrops patter down on the glass window.
I love that deep dark smell of wet dug up soil.
The trees are slender, streets warned of wild
Heaps of devotees line up before the deity
Religion is beyond my scope of understanding.
Nature, poetry, psychology are my forte
Naivety, gullible, innocent some synonym.
The hills are crowned with a wisp of white
Each curve shape shifting every second.
∞ 12.12.2019

147. Chaîne de mots

• 173 •

Window view
Weekend blues
Hot coffee brew
Pigeons sweet coo.
Window view
Winter flu
Kings' askew
Plan a coup
Window view
Sunday stew
Off with the shoe
Oh sing to me Babalu!
∞ 22.12.2019

148. Lever les yeux

Light cuts the hills,
the mountain
Rims the rays.
The sky peeps through
the lush green
breaks the clouds.

Up is the world
Not to miss,
Down below
Feet affirm & stiff.
Slip & fall
You must.
Look up look up look up!

Darling, the universe is you
You are the cosmos.
Start from below you will
Don't stop the climb
All the way to the top.
∞ 13.1.2020

149. Effervescence

It's early morn
Pitch black, hearts torn
The ghosts whispering
Has it been so long?

The silent screeching
Leaves crunching
Toes curling, hair raising
White mist swirls.

Shadows shape shift.
Winds directionlessly swift
Tick tock, there goes another day
Flip flop, another year
Bang - clang, another decade.

Time slips through
Sand in my hand
Grab what you can
The effervescence.
∞ 16.1.2020

150. Paradise

A man stands still
Middle of a shallow gurgle
Watching the red flags
Of a 100 something BC temple
Rustling again the gushes
Transport prayers to the heavens.

~

The silhouette dotted
With ruffled heads
Of coniferous tree tops
Yellow darlings on terraces
Dancing to the tunes
Of mountain owls

~

Scarecrow shadows
Metamorphosing
Branched arms grab out
Through dusky darkness
Mere flicker to guide.

~

I stand still
Middle of a gorgeous gorge
Watching the snow tops

Glide in & out of the fluffs
Wondering yet again how
We never deserved this paradise.
∞ 18.1.2020

151. Ci vediamo

Three little sibs
Burrow near the stream
Youngest giving out
Animated orders
Queen mother looks below
Sunbath on the roof.
Shivering men share their
Surreptitious smoke
Watching burning fumes
Blend into the dusky sky.

~

Silhouette's studded tonight
A mirror to the starry sky
Embers blown back to life
Send cinders flying
Ash-flakes fall
Musty pyre odors
Inferno smolders.

~

Wave a silly goodbye
Company of the cat
Waddle back indoors
Snuggle the coverlets.

Goodbye oh snowy
Au revoir my darlings
Ci rivedremo presto!
∞19.1.2020

152. Intangible Powers

Let me attempt to give you
An amalgamation of words
To describe the gufhas and leopards.
Let me try to tell you of the ruffled head
Of the old vagabond with his bindle
Or the uniformed girls
Giving their morning offerings
To the temple at the footsteps of their home.

All the colloquy complied
Won't sufice to sketch
The color of the rocks
That disturb the river
The white effervescence.
Or tree that shades
The mighty mountain
Or the majestic queen of the snows
Having her morning sun bath
Over shadowing all around her.
You need to see this
With your own eyes
You need to stand
At the edge of the cliff

Be the centre of this universe
Surround sounds of
The Himalayan sparrows
The gushing rivulet
The rustle bustle
Of the snow laden leaves
Quiet pitter patter of the hilly folk.

Let me attempt to give you
An amalgamation of words
To describe the mandirs & wildcats.
Let me try to enunciate the names of places
I couldn't even dream of & yet
Here I am
In the middle of the waters
A temple on stilts
Gratitude to an intangible power
The life I am living.
∞ 20.1.2020

153. Ramblings of a Writer 0202

Heart racing
Palm sweating
Numerous anxious reasons
Book in hand
Words flowing
Singing poetry of deodars
Birds and cicadas

~

Was I always like this
Did the air get me high
Or do Mr. Bond and I
Ail with the same
Mountain sickness?
Nimble fingers glide
Linking letter by letter
Drawing a photograph
Beauty that lay

~

Repetitive might be
Though different they are
Just as the misty fog
Swirls in my head

Heart aching
Goodbyes pending
Numerous wistful beings
∞ 2.2.2020

154. Old Town

Quaint places
Smelly faces
Feet sore
Eyes soar.
Saffron covers
Secret lovers
Evening song
Walk so long.
Small beings
Sight seeings
Never too old
A tad too cold.
Dharamshalas
Daisy malas
Blind beggars
Quiet eager.
Magnificent moon
Imprudent baffoon
Sun down
Old town.
∞ 8.2.2020

155. An Evening by the River

Curl in your toes
Chilling soft stream
Small waves on the surface
Fishes adventurous.

Sprinkle your fingers
Twinkle & gleam
Small pebbles under water
Moss covered totter.

Wipe away your sins
Ripe sun beam
Small creatures dive about
Free, up & out.
∞ 01.03.2020

156. Gyrus

Repdigited dates
Amorphous shapes.
Endless escapes
Inevitable escalates
Restless anticipates.
Repetitive gyrates.
∞ 3.3.2020

157. Sunset 222

Murmuration of cotton candy
Babbling of silly crows
Sinking of the setting sun
Auf Wiedersehen
To a beautiful day done
∞ 16.3.2020

158. Safe Haven

The hills have a halo today
A white sheen
Outline peeks.
The cuppa simmers
Early summer morn
Remanence days gone.

The cafe around the corner
A place quiet
Blue and white
Cocooned under canopies
Limited menu and people
Busiest cu de sac of the city.

The literary cafe down hill
A quaint house
Stacked with books
Unending food & drink
Rapidly recycling guests
Touristy turn of town.
The rocks by the bay
Shades of white & grey
Crowded couples scattered

Leap from stone to sleet
Waves gently lick our feet
Glorious sunset skyline

The cushion in the corner
Behind the bookshelf
By the balcony
Raindrops trickling in
A cup of coffee
My favourite story.

The suitcases at the door
A beautiful home to leave
Hoarded books, treasured tales
Everything placed with care
Warm awkward embrace
Universes' love encased.
∞ 31.3.2020

159. Alliteration 441

Glorious greatness
Magnificent moments
Brilliant blues
A second too soon.
Effulgent immensity
Occasional opulence
Heavenly hues
Many a boon.
∞14.4.2020

160. Rebellious Sky

Silly slithering clouds
Mind of their own
Swift drift, float away.
Silly celestial shrouds
Body none at all
Float gloat, fly away.
Silly summer crowds
Soulful sighs prevail
Fly cry, sail away.
∞13.6.2020

161. Transition Words

Parch

Exsiccate

Thirst

Hunger

Passion

Avidite

Saturate

Pyre

Inundate

∞ 26.6.2020

162. Portray

Sit here all day
Clouds drift away
Twigs gently sway
Knotty wind play
Please oh please stay
∞ 8.7.2020

163. Close Your Eyes

Crackling crickets
Thundering clouds
Booming barrages
Puddling ploughs.

Cricketing croakers
Swinging shrouds
Blaring boomboxes
The world aloud.

Croaking canoes
Surging crowds
Boxed up babies
Limited allow(ed)
∞ 19.7.2020

164. Arrival

Curtains breathe blue
Lines all askew
Clouds blow bellow
Thunder grum growl.

Metaphors that mean
Nothing as seen
Twisted curvy tails
Wait, steady sails.

Who what when where
'Nything to care
Waves lap at toes
Hideaway coves.

Seashore shimmer
Lights are dimmer
Sail steady home
Escape dread storm.
∞ 30.08.2020

165. Alliteration 103

Sleepy smiles
Squirrel scrabble
Senile squabble
And
Serendipitous
Salmon sun sets.
∞ 03.10.2020

166. Toasts

To views that never age,
the disguised dog - sage.
To rivers that never move,
that dark dingy cove.
To winters that never delude,
Hours and hours to brood.
To time that never stops
Seamless azure pops.
∞ 04.12.2020

167. Rainbow

It's a beautiful day
To be alive
To smile
To rejoice

It's a gorgeously sunny day
Hair down
Cheshire smile
For poses cliché

Today of all days
Is perfectly splendid
For you are
Breathing
Walking &
Seeing all the world
∞ 09.12.2020

168. Sunset Silhouette

Star lights to remember
Sunsets to forget
Dream worlds to relive
Fleeting lives of silhouette (s)
∞ 5.2.2021

169. Que sera sera

Watch the play, play out.
A set I've seen before.
A place for everything
A thing for every place.

Place my foot into footprints
Laugh a laugh, laughed before
The hourglass trickles sand
The sand tickles glass.

Move forward, look ahead
Leave behind reminiscent hearts
Photograph for memories
Memorise those photos.

Our lives drawn out
Destiny and karma
As 2 and 2 make four
This is forever more.
∞10.03.2021

170. Luminosities

Azure dreams fulfilled
Sphere shattering shades.
Dip my toes into clear oceans
Swim dazzle mazzle phase.

Royal dreams gratified
With dyes to die for.
Open my eyes into clear waters
Silence hustle bustle shore.

Cyanic dreams actualised
With seductive sceneries.
Lay back the floor boards
Look the luminosities wait to be devoured.
∞15.3.2021

171. Prudent

Exotic flowers amongst whispy whites,
Infinite horizons all within sight.
Treacherous roots deep within
How does it matter good, bad, sin.

White crosses contrast vermilion smears
Misty mountains forever in clear
Perilous pillars stand straight, tall
How does it matter, trouble befall.

Conspicuous sounds from coniferous trees
Floating through the brisk breeze
Ravenous ravine gape below
Watch your step, careful, slow.

∞ 11.4.2021

172. Nomad

Suitcase life
D'nerve nomad
Half the year
A blur.

Wee wounds vice
Subtle sighs, sad
Five full months
A slur.

Luggage lies
Sloven sully clad
One fifty days
Recur?
∞ 20.5.2021

173. Capture

Click capture emotion
Sunset smiles, hilly highs
Singular destruction.

Duck evade devotion
Milky mine's, sandy sighs
Dual interjections.

Snap shutter motion
Stary skies, windy whines
Collective resurrection.
∞01.06.2021

174. Sun Chasers

The moon in the bright blue sky
Mingling amongst the wips
Watching over the world
Chasing the sun all along.

The moon in the monstrous milkys
Ushering through the asteroids
Squinting in the cosmic storm
Chasing the sun all along.

The moon in the dark night shade
Waltzing amongst the stars
Wide eyed over the terrene
Chasing the sun all along.
∞ 21.7.2021

175. Summer Moon

Blasphemous Buck Moons
Dwindle dew drops
Swerving solitary sky.

Hallowed Hay Moons
Droughty day dies
Peeking pious July.

Thirsty Thunder Moons
Dreadful dire straits
Swindling serendipity sighs.
∞ 24.7.2021

176. Story

• 207 •

Write you a story
One day I will
One that moves you
Stays with you
Keeps you thinking
Hours after The End
Write you a story
One day I will.
∞ 05.12.2021

177. '21 The Conclusion

Catch the evening sky
Pirouetting ripples of purple
Perfect brew for a storm
Splendid time for g'bye.

Catch the night sky
Studded rhinestone white
Perfect calm don't conform
Splendid time don't be shy.

Catch the mornin' sky
Canorous streaks of bright
Perfect melange of wit & charm
Splendid time for Oh Hello - Hi.
∞ 31.12.2021

178. Rhymeless Muttering on a Highway

Dawn sky - a threatening orange
Single green parrot sneaks away
Two mynas , oh lucky me.
Wobbly young man, confused cow
Sway speeding segway
Flashing hazard light
Lane swooshing little cars.
Village smells, lopsided haystack
balances lopsided mini lorry
There goes the morning sky
Brilliant chameleon colors
Never ending beautiful roads
Deep bass, blast my ear
Hair splaying, frills fluttering winds
Earphones dangle, middle aged bloke
Videotaping his drive.
Aunty ji zooming on her Luna
16 wheeler lorry tugs along logs of lumber
Heavy heart sighs, passengers sweetly snooze
Flamingo pink goes the sunset
Now old man and compelled cows
Middle of the highway

Drivers mother calls for an ETA
New friends chatter away
Little girls & their day of freedom
Simple are the purest joys of life.
∞ 6.3.2022

179. Simple Joys

Swaying flowers
By the ripples on the pond.
Dancing monkeys
On the temple roof tops.
Blessings strangers
Selfless love, blind faith.
Oh how simple are these joys.

Swaying flowers
By the ripples on the pond.
Smiling pedestrians
Running amok little boys.
Streaming sunrays
Ripping through dark clouds
Oh how simple are these joys.
∞ 19.6.2022

180. Writer's Longing

I want to write something profound
To make you think and pound
About the depths of life and despair
I wonder if there is anything left to share.

I want to create something beautiful
With mere words as my tool(s)
About the joys & sorrows we perceive
I wonder if there's anything left to seize.

One day
I will manifest something magnificent
In this world I shall leave a mark, a dent
About the stories & tales of my life
I hope you enjoy these lullabies.
∞ 1.03.2023